Unsolved!

MYSTERIES OF THE MIND

Kathryn Walker

based on original text by Brian Innes

Crabtree Publishing Company

www.crabtreebooks.com

Crabtree Publishing Company

www.crabtreebooks.com

Author: Kathryn Walker
   based on original text by Brian Innes
Project editor: Kathryn Walker
Picture researcher: Rachel Tisdale
Managing editor: Miranda Smith
Art director: Jeni Child
Design manager: David Poole
Editorial director: Lindsey Lowe
Children's publisher: Anne O'Daly
Editor: Molly Aloian
Proofreader: Crystal Sikkens
Crabtree editorial director: Kathy Middleton
Production coordinator: Katherine Berti
Prepress technician: Katherine Berti

Cover: An illustration of the human
brain representing the concept of ideas
and the power of the mind.

Photographs:
Corbis: William Campbell/Sygma: p. 26
Discovery Books: p. 17
Fortean Picture Library: p. 7, 22
Istockphoto: dmitryphotos: p. 6;
   skodonnell: p. 19
Mary Evans Picture Library/SPR: p. 16
NASA: p. 25
Shutterstock: Vladimir Daragan: p. 27;
   Jim Feliciano: p. 12; iDesign: front
   cover; O.V.D.: p. 20; Bruce Rolff: p. 30;
   Forrest L. Smith III: p. 15; Alexey
   Stiop: p. 10; Kheng Guan Toh: p. 5;
   watercolourz: p. 23
Topfoto: p. 8 (right and left), 11, 21;
   Elmer R. Gruber/Fortean: p. 29

Every effort has been made to trace the
owners of copyrighted material.

Library and Archives Canada Cataloguing in Publication

Walker, Kathryn
   Mysteries of the mind / Kathryn Walker ; based on original
text by Brian Innes.

(Unsolved!)
Includes index.
ISBN 978-0-7787-4149-7 (bound).--ISBN 978-0-7787-4162-6 (pbk.)

   1. Extrasensory perception--Juvenile literature.
2. Psychokinesis--Juvenile literature. I. Title.
II. Series: Unsolved! (St. Catharines, Ont.)

BF1321.W29 2009   j133.8   C2009-901926-4

Library of Congress Cataloging-in-Publication Data

Walker, Kathryn.
  Mysteries of the mind / Kathryn Walker ; based on original text by
Brian Innes.
    p. cm. -- (Unsolved!)
  Includes index.
  ISBN 978-0-7787-4162-6 (pbk. : alk. paper)
-- ISBN 978-0-7787-4149-7 (reinforced library binding : alk. paper)
  1. Extrasensory perception--Juvenile literature. 2. Psychokinesis--
Juvenile literature. I. Innes, Brian. II. Title. III. Series.

  BF1321.W36 2010
  133.8--dc22

2009013080

Crabtree Publishing Company
www.crabtreebooks.com   1-800-387-7650

Published in Canada
Crabtree Publishing
616 Welland Ave.
St. Catharines, ON
L2M 5V6

Published in the United States
Crabtree Publishing
PMB16A
350 Fifth Ave., Suite 3308
New York, NY 10118

Published by CRABTREE PUBLISHING COMPANY in 2010

Contents

Sixth Sense?

...Some people seem to have amazing mind powers.

In December, 1971, artist Ingo Swann sat in a room in New York. A tray was suspended several feet above his head. There were objects on the tray, but Swann could not see them.

Swann began to sketch a picture that came into his mind. He drew a shape with some odd markings he did not understand. Then someone turned the sketch around and the markings made sense. They spelled out the name of a soda. Swann had drawn a soda can that was on the tray—upside down!

Some people, like Ingo Swann, can pick up information in a way that we cannot explain. There are five human **senses**: sight, touch, smell, hearing, and taste. But it is as if these people are using an extra sense—a sixth sense. The more scientific name for this is **extrasensory perception (ESP)**.

>> **sense**—A way in which we know what is happening around us

People with ESP are able to use something other than the usual five senses. This is sometimes called a "sixth sense" or "the third eye."

>> **extrasensory perception (ESP)**—The ability to get information using unusual mind powers   **5**

How did it happen?

How did Swann know what was on the tray? The chances of him guessing correctly were very small. Did he see the soda can reflected on an object in the room? If not, then maybe he was using ESP.

This can work in different ways. If one of the scientists working on the test knew what was on the tray, Swann might have been able to read his or her thoughts. This kind of ESP is known as **telepathy**.

According to Swann, this is not what happened. He said he felt his mind float up to the ceiling and look down on the tray.

This is a type of ESP called "remote viewing." The word "remote" describes something that is at a distance, or is controlled from a distance. It seemed that Swann looked at the object on the tray without moving from his seat.

"[Swann] said he felt his mind float up to the ceiling and look down on the tray."

Being able to read someone else's thoughts is a type of ESP called telepathy.

>> **telepathy**—Mind reading, or sending thoughts from one person's mind to another

Studying ESP

Centuries ago, most people believed in what we now call ESP. Then, during the 1800s, scientists in many countries began to laugh at these ideas. They refused to believe in things they could not explain.

In many cases, these scientists were right. There were people who were clearly pretending to have special powers. However, there were other cases that could not be explained away.

A number of people formed groups, or societies, for psychic studies. To be "**psychic**" means being sensitive to forces beyond the natural world.

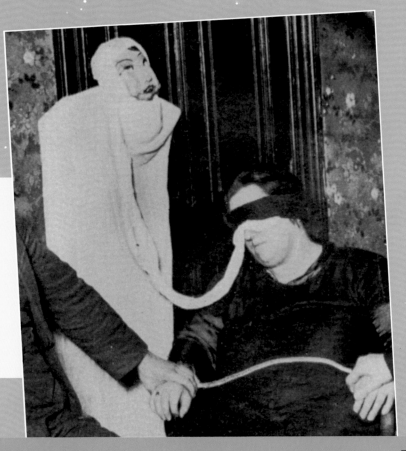

This photo was meant to show a woman using special powers to make contact with the spirits of dead people. Could anyone have thought it was real?

More Mind Messages

...There have been some amazing tales of ESP.

Upton Sinclair was a famous American **author**. In 1930, he published a book titled *Mental Radio*. In it, he described experiments in telepathy carried out with his wife, Mary.

Sinclair describes sitting in his study with the door shut and drawing whatever came into his mind. Several rooms away, his wife would try to draw the same picture, using telepathy. Out of 290 drawings, 65 exactly matched her husband's. She partly matched 155 more. Only 70 were failures.

Sinclair also said that his wife could sense how people were feeling, even when the people were hundreds of miles (km) away. He wrote: "I tell you—and because it is so important, I put it in capital letters: TELEPATHY HAPPENS!"

The author Upton Sinclair is shown here along with sketches (far right) from one of his experiments. The sketches on the left side are those that Sinclair made. On the right side are sketches that his wife Mary drew at the same time, using telepathy.

>> **author**—A person who writes something, such as a book, a play, or similar work

"I tell you—and because it is so important, I put it in capital letters: TELEPATHY HAPPENS!"

Here is a love story which seems to go wrong, the hearts being turned to opposition (Figs. 126, 126a):

Fig. 126

Fig. 126a

Here is the flag, made simpler—"e pluribus unum!" (Figs. 127, 127a):

Fig. 127

Fig. 127a

Here is a cow, as seen by the cubists. Comment: "Something sending out long lines from it" (Figs. 128, 128a):

Fig. 128

Fig. 128a

Telegraph wires, apparently seen as waves in the ether (Figs. 129, 129a):

Fig. 129

Fig. 129a

Power in the hands

Another type of ESP is called psychometry. People with this power hold or touch objects. They can then explain where it came from, who owned it, and details about the owner.

People who can do this are called psychometrists. They say that the information comes to them as pictures in the mind, feelings, or sounds. It is as if the object records information and the person is able to play back the recording.

A psychometrist is able to receive information through the fingers or hands.

Touching the past

George McMullen was a psychometrist. In 1971, he did an experiment with Norman J. Emerson, an expert in Native American history.

Emerson handed McMullen a **fragment** of clay. After holding it, McMullen said it was part of a pipe used in Native American ceremonies. This was true. Then he described how the pipe had been made and drew a picture of the complete object. Again, he was right.

"It is as if the object records information and the person is able to play back the recording."

>> **fragment**—A small piece of something

*Gerard Croiset is seen here in 1969. He is studying a photograph of a **kidnapped** woman in an attempt to help police find her.*

Psychic detective

Gerard Croiset was a Dutch psychometrist. During the 1940s and 1950s, he was often asked to help the police solve crimes and find missing people.

On one occasion, Croiset was given a piece of clothing belonging to a missing girl. By holding it, he knew that she had been murdered. He told the police where to find her body and gave them details of how she was murdered. He even told them the name of the girl's murderer.

Croiset became famous for his skills. However, in the 1960s and 1970s, many of his attempts to find missing people failed.

How Strange...

Gerard Croiset's son had the same ability as his father. He once helped find the bodies of two murdered girls.

Mind travel

Patrick H. Price was a retired police commissioner from Burbank, California. He said he often used remote viewing to catch criminals. During the 1970s, two scientists in California performed some tests on Price. They wanted to find out if he really did have special powers.

In one test, a scientist was given a long list of places. He then had to choose which ones to drive to. Nobody else would know where the scientist was going. Price stayed behind. His job was to try to describe the **locations** that the scientist was visiting.

Price scored well in these tests. His descriptions often matched the locations. Once, he even named the building that the scientist was visiting. It was the Hoover Tower at Stanford University.

This is the Hoover Tower at Stanford University, California. Price named it correctly during an experiment.

>> **location**—A place or site where something is

A watery spot

On one occasion, Price described a location as having two pools of water—one circular and one rectangular—with a concrete building nearby. This description matched the location. It was a swimming pool complex in a park.

Price went on to describe some water storage tanks. He also saw machinery in the pools. Price said he thought the location was a **waterworks**. The scientists thought he was wrong.

Backward in time

About 20 years later, one of the scientists, Russell Targ, came across a photo of the swimming pool area as it was in 1913. At that time, it was a waterworks. The water tanks were in the photo, exactly where Price said they were. It seemed like he was looking back in time.

When Price saw two water tanks, such as this one, he had been looking back in time.

"It seemed that [Price] had been looking back in time."

New Science

...In the 1920s, scientists began to take an interest in psychical research.

The people who set up the early tests for ESP were not usually scientists. They did not know how to design **foolproof** tests. It was easy for people to get good results from tricks.

Scientist Dr. William McDougall believed that research into ESP was important. He thought it would help create a clear picture of how the human mind worked. In 1927, McDougall began work at Duke University, North Carolina. Dr. Joseph Banks Rhine joined him.

The Zener test

Dr. Rhine asked scientist Karl Zener to design some cards to use in his ESP experiments. Zener produced a set of five cards, each with a simple shape or **symbol**. There were 25 cards in a pack—five of each design. During a test, the pack was shuffled. The person being tested had to guess the order of cards in the pack. This would test for ESP.

>> **foolproof**—Designed to make it difficult for mistakes or misuse to happen

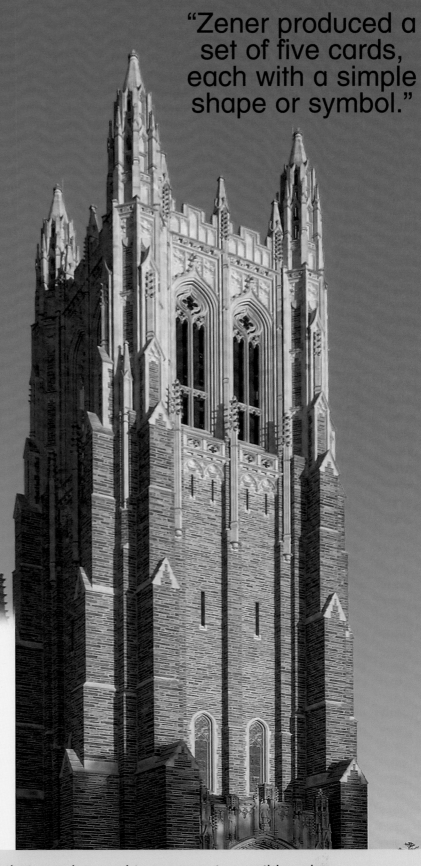

"Zener produced a set of five cards, each with a simple shape or symbol."

At Duke University (right), Dr. William McDougall set up studies to test for ESP. Above is the set of cards that Karl Zener designed for ESP experiments.

>> **symbol**—A shape or sign that may be used to represent something else

Testing time

Dr. Rhine performed experiments using the Zener cards. The scientists determined that someone guessing by chance could name at least five of the 25 cards correctly. A correct answer was called a "**hit**." But if someone regularly got more than five hits, it could not be by chance.

Rhine tried this test on a student named Adam J. Linzmayer. Time and time again Linzmayer got nine hits out of 25. Then, after a while, his number of hits began to drop.

Amazing results

Another student named Hubert E. Pearce, Jr., did even better. He scored as high as 13 hits out of the possible 25. Out of a total of 750 cards, Hubert scored 261 hits. This could not be happening by chance.

Preventing boredom

Rhine found that when people became tired or bored with the tests, their scores dropped. He tried to make the tests more exciting. He offered Pearce $100 for each hit he made. Pearce got all 25 cards correct!

"...when people became tired or bored with the tests, their scores dropped."

Dr. Rhine was one of the first scientists to seriously study ESP.

>> **hit**—A successful result

After carrying out thousands of tests, Rhine wrote about his results. This forced other scientists to accept the importance of his work. The Institute for **Parapsychology** was set up near Duke University. Parapsychology means the study of ESP and other unusual powers of the mind.

A long way to go

High scores in ESP testing are rare. Good results need to be repeated over and over to prove that ESP exists. Otherwise, scientists think that the high scores could occur by chance, mistake, or through trickery.

Testing with Zener cards can now be done using computers.

Mind Over Matter

...Can people make things happen just by the power of thought?

Card players may tell you that, if they think hard enough, they can sometimes make the cards fall as they want them to. Some dice players say the same about dice. Is it possible for lifeless objects to be affected by thought?

This ability has interested researchers for years. It is called **psychokinesis** or PK. The name comes from two ancient Greek words that together mean "mind movement."

Eusapia Palladino was an Italian woman born in 1854. She was able to move objects, such as tables, without touching them. Palladino's powers puzzled researchers. Many thought that she did have mysterious powers; but they also thought she sometimes used tricks.

*Using mind powers to make objects float or rise up in the air is a type of psychokinesis called **levitation**.*

>> **psychokinesis (PK)**—The ability to make objects move using only the mind

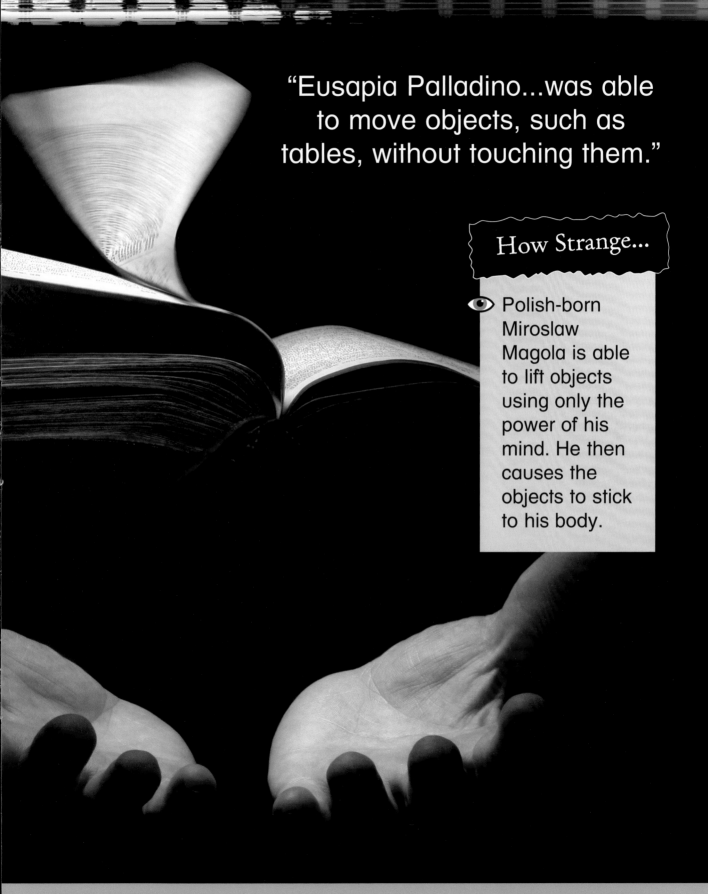

"Eusapia Palladino...was able to move objects, such as tables, without touching them."

How Strange...

👁 Polish-born Miroslaw Magola is able to lift objects using only the power of his mind. He then causes the objects to stick to his body.

Bending spoons

Psychokinesis not only means making objects move. It means using the power of the mind to control objects in other ways, too. For example, some people can bend metal objects without force or through gentle touch.

Probably the most famous person in modern times who claims to have this power is Israeli-born Uri Geller.

A famous act

At first, Geller used his skills to entertain people on stage. In the early 1970s, he attracted attention in the United States and appeared on television. Across the world, millions of amazed viewers watched him make spoons and keys bend just by stroking them. He also claimed to be able to stop and start watches and clocks with his special powers.

After the program, many viewers called the television studio to say that they had found bent **flatware** in their own homes. Some also said that stopped clocks suddenly started up again. A lot of people claimed that they, too, could bend flatware.

"...millions of amazed viewers watched him make spoons and keys bend..."

In the 1970s, many people were fascinated by the idea of being able to bend spoons through the power of the mind.

>> **flatware**—Knives, forks, and spoons used for eating

Uri Geller is seen here with his Cadillac. It is decorated with thousands of pieces of bent flatware.

True or false?

Some scientists who tested Geller's abilities were impressed. But it was later suggested that their tests had not been set up carefully enough. This meant Geller could have cheated.

Geller has been accused of being nothing more than a **stage magician**. People have pointed out that well-known stage tricks can achieve the same results. Geller himself has admitted to sometimes using tricks in his performances, as well as his own powers. However, many people still believe that he is a man with very special powers.

How Strange...

- Uri Geller claims that he discovered his powers when he was a child.

- In one television show, Geller appeared to cause a fork to bend without touching it.

The mystery of Nina

Nina Kulagina was born in 1926 in the **Soviet Union**, which was a group of states that included Russia. In the 1960s, news of Kulagina's special powers caused great excitement. She seemed able to move small objects without touching them.

Soviet scientists tested Kulagina. They filmed her moving objects, such as matchboxes and pens. In the films, she moves objects by staring at them or holding her hands over them. One time, Kulagina is said to have once used her powers to stop the beating of a frog's heart.

These events were reported at a time of distrust and competition between the Soviet Union and the United States. Some people wondered if the reports were really true.

Here Nina Kulagina is looking into a camera. She is trying to make a picture form on the film using only mind power.

How Strange...

- Doctors said that using her powers left Nina Kulagina exhausted and ill.

- Kulagina claimed that when she was a child, objects would move around her when she was feeling angry.

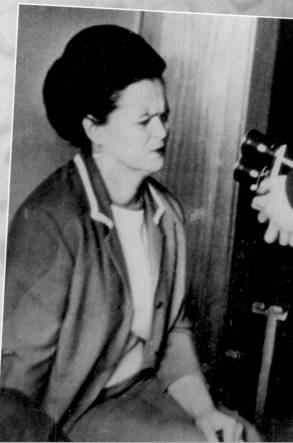

>> **Soviet Union**—A large group of states that included Russia, but no longer exists

Dr. Rhine wanted to see if it was possible to turn up particular numbers on dice using mind power.

The dice machine

Back in the 1930s, Dr. Joseph Banks Rhine (see page 14) of Duke University performed experiments with dice. He wanted to see if it was possible to make dice turn up particular numbers by thought alone.

Rhine built a special dice-tumbling machine. The machine made sure that nothing affected how the dice fell. In tests, students were asked which numbers would turn up on the dice when the machine stopped.

By chance, it is possible to get five guesses out of 12 correct. But in Rhine's tests, the successes were higher. Rhine thought his results showed that the mind could **influence** the way dice fell.

"Rhine thought his results showed that the mind could influence the way dice fell."

>> **influence**—To affect or alter

Project Stargate

...In 1970, reports about the use of ESP caused alarm.

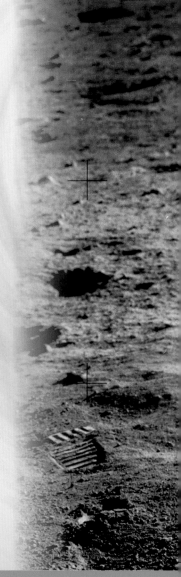

The Cold War was a time of **hostility** between the Soviet Union (see page 22) and the United States. It lasted from 1945 until 1991. The Soviet Union and the United States never actually fought during this time, but they did not trust each other.

The two powers competed with each other in space exploration. The race to get people and **satellites** into space was called the "space race." Each side tried to keep what they were doing a secret. Then, in 1970, a report said that Soviet astronauts were being trained in ESP. It said that the astronauts were using telepathy in space.

The U.S. government worried that ESP could be used to discover U.S. secrets. They put money into a project to test ESP and how it might be used. The project was called Project Stargate.

>> **hostility**—Unfriendliness or behavior like that of an enemy

"The two powers competed with each other in space exploration."

How Strange...

- 👁 About 15 people with ESP powers worked on Project Stargate.

- 👁 One of the aims of the project was to gather information on U.S. enemies.

In 1969, the United States won the race to put the first men on the Moon. This photograph shows astronaut Buzz Aldrin walking on the Moon's surface.

Success stories

People working on Project Stargate used remote viewing to try to find out information. They used the powers of the mind to see what was happening in other places.

One of the men working on the project was Joe McMoneagle. In 1979, he was given a photo of a huge building in the Soviet Union. McMoneagle was asked to find out what was going on inside the building.

Using remote viewing, McMoneagle saw that the Soviets were building a new type of **submarine**. He made drawings of what he saw. McMoneagle said the submarine would be launched four months later. In January, 1980, he was proved right.

"Using remote viewing, McMoneagle saw that the Soviets were building a new type of submarine."

Joe McMoneagle, pictured here, was one of the first to join Project Stargate.

>> **submarine**—A type of ship that can travel underwater

This is the city of Padua in Italy. It was here that General James Dozier was held prisoner in 1982.

Missing person

In 1982, General James Dozier of the U.S. Army was kidnapped in Italy. Through remote viewing, McMoneagle correctly described the apartment where General Dozier was being held and its location in the Italian city of Padua. However, the Italian police may have already found General Dozier by the time McMoneagle's information reached them.

End of Stargate

Stargate had many failures, too. McMoneagle said that they were successful about 15 to 20 percent of the time. But he pointed out that many other systems used to gather information were less successful. The project was put in the hands of the **C.I.A.** They decided it was a waste of money and closed it down in 1995.

How Strange...

One of the early tasks for Project Stargate was to help the C.I.A. find a Soviet aircraft that had crashed in Africa. A remote viewer was able to tell them exactly where to find it.

Is There An Explanation?

...The human mind still holds some mysteries.

Could there really be a sixth sense? We use eyes for sight, ears for hearing, tongues for taste, noses for smell, and skin for touch. If there is a sixth sense, what body part is being used?

Some people suggest that there is a part deep inside the brain where people experience the sixth sense. Some people believe that once, long ago, everyone used this sense. Now that people no longer need special powers to survive, many of us have simply forgotten how to use it. Or perhaps, people with special powers just use the five normal senses. They might simply be better at using them than the rest of us.

Some people who have studied ESP and PK think there may be an unknown **force** around us that causes psychic events to happen. But no one has yet found a way of proving it exists.

How Strange...

Many people report that they have had at least one ESP experience in their lives. This often seems to happen after an upsetting event.

>> **force**—An energy or power

This picture, titled The **Aura**, *was painted by Ingo Swann. An aura is said to be a type of misty glow surrounding a person. People who see auras say that we all have one. Not everyone can see them, however.*

>> **aura**—A glow said to surround living things, caused by a force from inside them

A lack of proof

Many people have studied ESP and psychokinesis. Some of these studies suggest that certain people do have **extraordinary** powers. However, tests have failed to prove this fact.

In some cases, this is because of how the tests have been carried out. If anyone can think of any possible way that a signal could have passed between people during testing, a good result is spoiled. Also, it has proved difficult to keep getting good results over and over again.

Strong beliefs

Therefore, we do not have firm proof that special powers, such as ESP, exist. We have no scientific explanation for them, either. But this does not stop people from believing that the mind really does have mysterious powers. Perhaps one day they will not be so mysterious.

"...we do not have firm proof that special powers, such as ESP, exist."

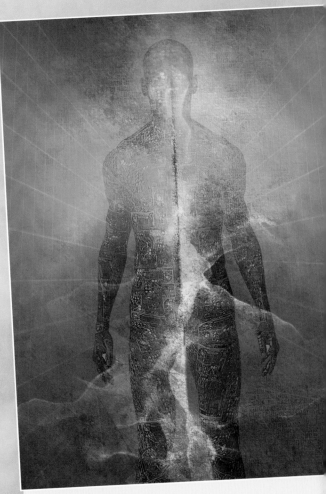

Maybe sometime in the future, we will discover that there is a force around us that causes psychic events.

>> **extraordinary**—Unusual or very strange

Glossary

aura A glow said to surround living things, caused by a force from inside them

author A person who writes something, such as a book, a play, or similar work

C.I.A. Central Intelligence Agency, a U.S. government organization for gathering information

extraordinary Unusual or very strange

extrasensory perception (ESP) The ability to get information using unusual mind powers

flatware Knives, forks, and spoons used for eating

foolproof Designed to make it difficult for mistakes or misuse to happen

force An energy or power

fragment A small piece of something

hit A successful result

hostility Unfriendliness or behavior like that of an enemy

influence To affect or alter

kidnapped Taken away and held by force

levitation When unusual powers of the mind cause a person or object to rise up in the air

location A place or site where something is

mental To do with the mind

parapsychology The study of powers of the mind that cannot be explained by science

psychic Being sensitive to forces beyond the natural world

psychokinesis (PK) The ability to make objects move using only the mind

satellite An object sent into space to travel around Earth or another planet

sense A way in which we know what is happening around us

Soviet Union A large group of states that included Russia, but no longer exists

stage magician Someone who entertains people with magic tricks or illusions

submarine A type of ship that can travel underwater

symbol A shape or sign that may be used to represent something else

telepathy Mind reading, or sending thoughts from one person's mind to another

waterworks A place for storing, cleaning, and providing water

Index

Further Reading

- Allen, Judy. *Unexplained: An Encyclopedia of Curious Phenomena, Strange Superstitions, and Ancient Mysteries*. Kingfisher, 2004.
- Herbst, Judith. *ESP,* "The Unexplained" series. Lerner Publications, 2004.
- Martin, Michael. *ESP: Extrasensory Perception*, "Edge Books" series. Capstone Press, 2006.
- Oxlade, Chris. *The Mysteries of ESP*, "Can Science Solve?" series. Heinemann, 2008.

Printed in the U.S.A.